THIS WORKBOOK BELONGS TO

_____

I AM A MASTERPIECE

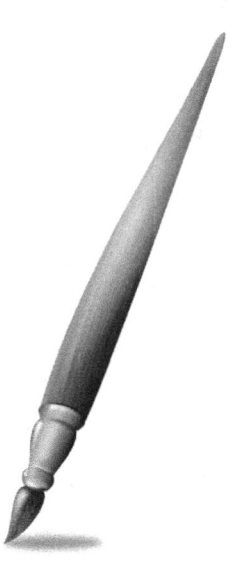

Printed in the United States of America

Keen Vision Publishing, LLC

www.keen-vision.com

ISBN: 978-1-955316-66-8

HELLO **MASTERPIECE,**

I love empowering people. One of my favorite ways to empower others is through encouraging positive self-esteem. There is so much power in our words. When others say good things about us, it makes us feel like we can conquer whatever we may be facing at the moment.

Sometimes, we will find ourselves without someone to encourage us. In these moments, we have to dig deep, find the right words, and motivate ourselves to keep going. This can be hard when we have low-self esteem. How do you build self-esteem? *I'm glad you asked.*

1. Understand that God calls you a **MASTERPIECE**. Yes, you. You are a **MASTERPIECE**! God's **MASTERPIECE**.

2. Learn about yourself. Know what you like, and things you do well.

3. Be kind to yourself. You're not perfect. No one is perfect...and that's okay! You must love yourself just the way you are. As you love yourself, you will get better in the areas of your life that need some work.

This workbook is filled with fun activities to help you build self-esteem. It doesn't matter your age or where you are in life, this workbook is a great tool for building great self-esteem. Before you dive into the fun, I want to tell you one more thing. I BELIEVE IN YOU! I hope that once you are complete this workbook, you believe in yourself too!

Enjoy,

"If you can imagine it, you can achieve it, if you can dream it, you can become it."

William Arthur Ward

SELF-ESTEEM

Self-esteem is how you feel about yourself. The way you feel about yourself can change from day to day. No one feels good about themselves all of the time. We all have good days and bad days. **What makes you feel bad?**

When we have positive self-esteem, we...

- Feel good about who we are
- Feel proud of what we can do
- Believe in ourselves even when we don't succeed the first time
- See our good qualities, such as being kind or capable
- Feel liked, loved, valued and respected
- Accept ourselves even when we make mistakes

What makes you feel good about yourself?

Having Positive self-esteem helps you feel confident about yourself and having negative self-esteem can hurt you and you don't feel confident. **On a scale of 0 to 10, how do you feel about yourself today?**

0	1	2	3	4	5	6	7	8	9	10
		(0-4)			(5-7)			(8-10)		
		Not too good			Okay			Confident		

If you're not feeling good, don't worry! The next pages are filled with more fun exercises to boost your self-esteem!

For we are God's masterpiece. He has created us anew in Christ Jesus, so we can do the good things he planned for us long ago.

Ephesians 2:10 (NLT)

MAS · TER · PIECE

/ˈmastərˌpēs/

noun

a work of outstanding artistry, skill, or workmanship.

You are a **MASTERPIECE** in God's eyes! Ephesians 2:10 (NLT) says, *"For we are God's* **MASTERPIECE.** *He has created us a new in Christ Jesus, so we can do the good things he planned for us long ago."*

What are three things that make you a
MASTERPIECE?

1.

2.

3.

One important key to success is self-confidence. An important key to self-confidence is preparation.

Arthur Ashe

MY **FAVORITE** THINGS

We all have things that we enjoy more than anything else. Write your favorite things! Draw a small picture that represents each thing you love!

Favorite Food

Favorite Type of Music

Favorite Song

Favorite Color

Favorite Ice Cream

Favorite Activity

Favorite Outfit

Favorite TV Show

Favorite Place to Be

Favorite Book

Favorite Subject in School

Favorite Person

So God created man in his own image, in the image of God he created him; male and female he created them.

Genesis 1:27 (ESV)

I'M **LOVING** ME

What are five things you love about yourself?

I praise you, for I am fearfully and wonderfully made. Wonderful are your works; my soul knows it very well.

Psalm 139:14 (ESV)

YOU ARE **SPECIAL!**

Unscramble the words below. Here's a hint: **These are words we can use to build positive self-esteem!** Flip the page over for answers, but no peeking!

uqunie _____

scplaie _____

ftig _____

atsr _____

elov _____

ritcfrie _____

gdoo _____

gamizn _____

tgear _____

liatbuefu _____

For I can do everything through Christ, who gives me strength.

Philippians 4:13 (NLT)

ACCOMPLISHMENTS

Everyone has skills and talents. Using your talents can help boost your Self-esteem. List special awards (certificates, trophies, or medals) you have received or accomplishments that make you proud!

Don't be afraid. Be focused. Be determined. Be hopeful. Be empowered.

Michelle Obama

BE **INSPIRED**

There are so many inspiring people in the world! They inspire us and help us believe that we can do anything! In the space below, **list 5 people who inspire you to be great!** Then, write two cool things you like about them!

1.

2.

3.

4.

5.

20 THINGS TO BOOST YOUR SELF-ESTEEM

1. Prayer
2. Read The Bible
3. Self-Esteem/Gratitude Journal
4. Vision/Dream Board
5. Positive Self-Talk
6. Self-Esteem Calendar
7. Exercise
8. Eat Healthy
9. Celebrate You
10. Read a Good Book
11. Spend time with people who make you feel good
12. Random Acts of Kindness
13. Forgive Yourself/Forgive Others
14. Try Something Exciting and New
15. Do your best, not perfection
16. Smile/Laugh Often
17. Volunteer
18. Do Chores
19. Control Your Temper
20. Complete *I am a Masterpiece* Workbook

YOU ARE
AMAZING

I tell you, you can pray for anything, and if you believe that you've received it, it will be yours.

Mark 11:24 (NLT)

TALK TO **GOD**

When you pray, you can talk to God about anything that is on your heart or mind...even your self-esteem. God hears you whenever you pray, it doesn't matter where you are or what time it is! He is always listening to you because you are His children and He cares for you. Use the space below to write a special prayer to God!

The thief's purpose is to steal and kill and destroy. My purpose is to give them a rich and satisfying life.

John 10:10 (NLT)

LET'S MAKE A
LIFE BOOK

Have you ever heard of a life book? It's a collection of your memories! You can include pictures, souvenirs, special notes, drawings, writings, or whatever you want! You can use your life book to record your history and the goals you have for the future. Grab some markers, crayons, a copy of your favorite pictures, stickers, or what ever you want to add in your life book! Use the next few pages to make your life book, or use of binder, photo album, or scrapbook!

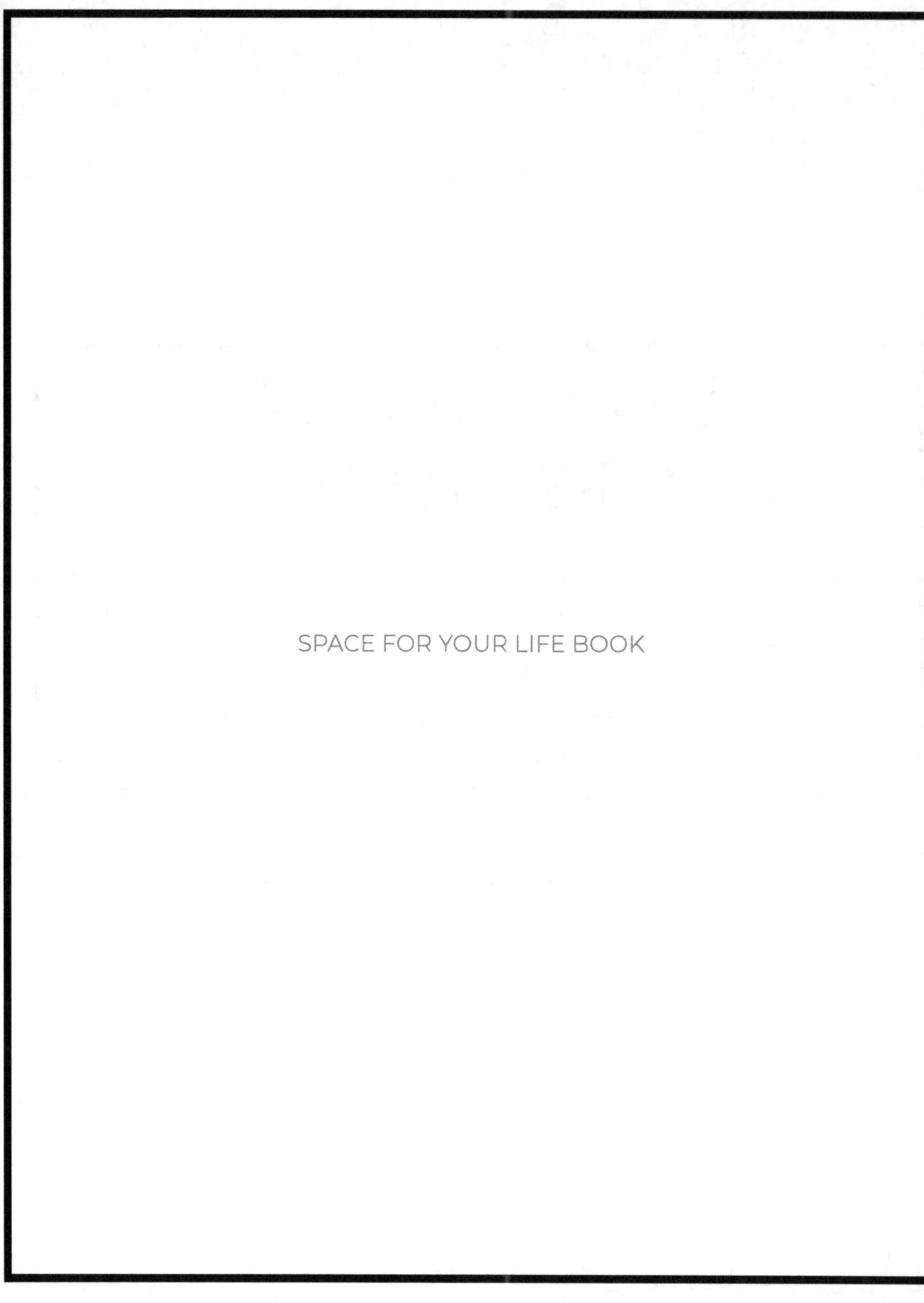

SPACE FOR YOUR LIFE BOOK

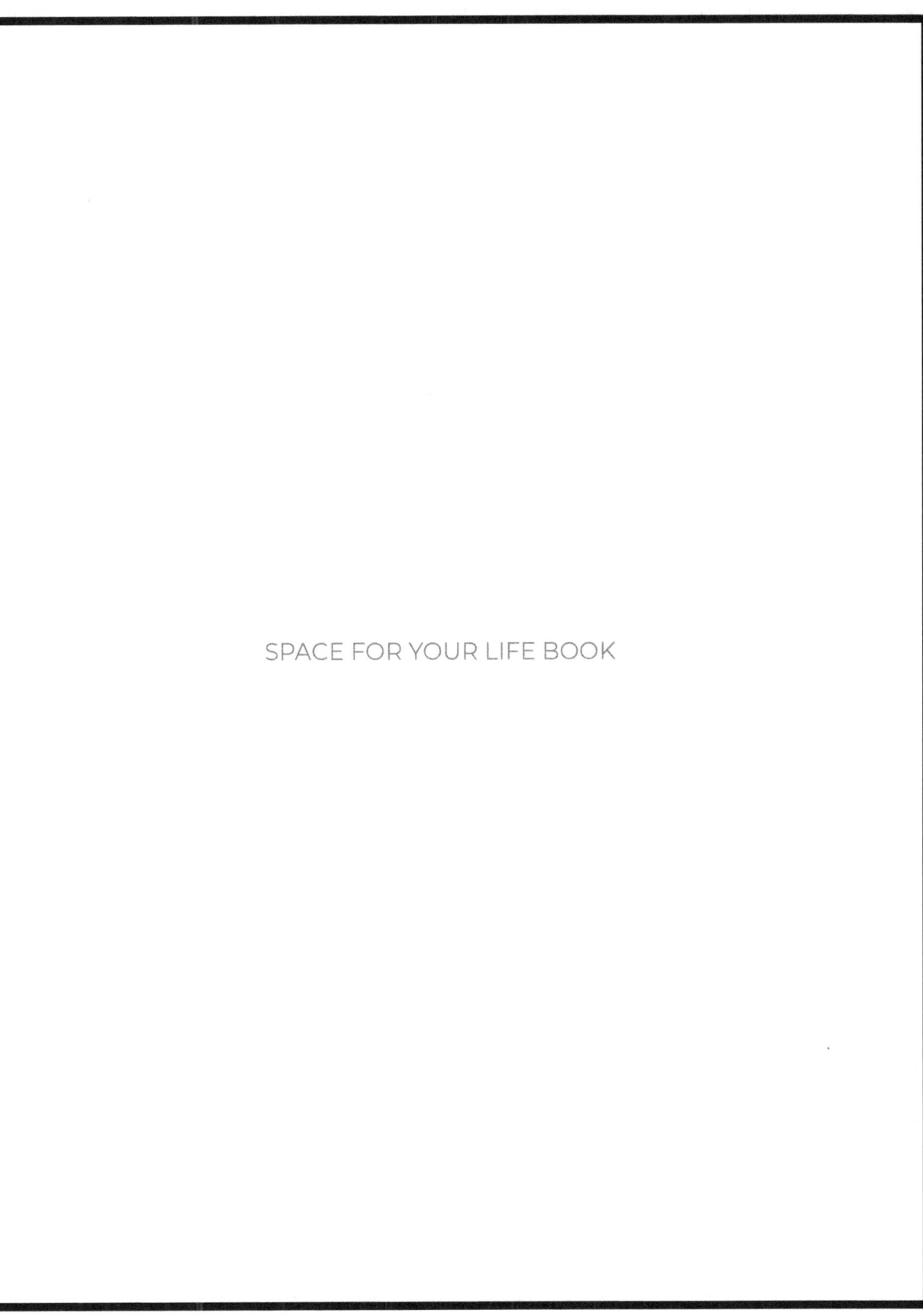

SPACE FOR YOUR LIFE BOOK

SPACE FOR YOUR LIFE BOOK

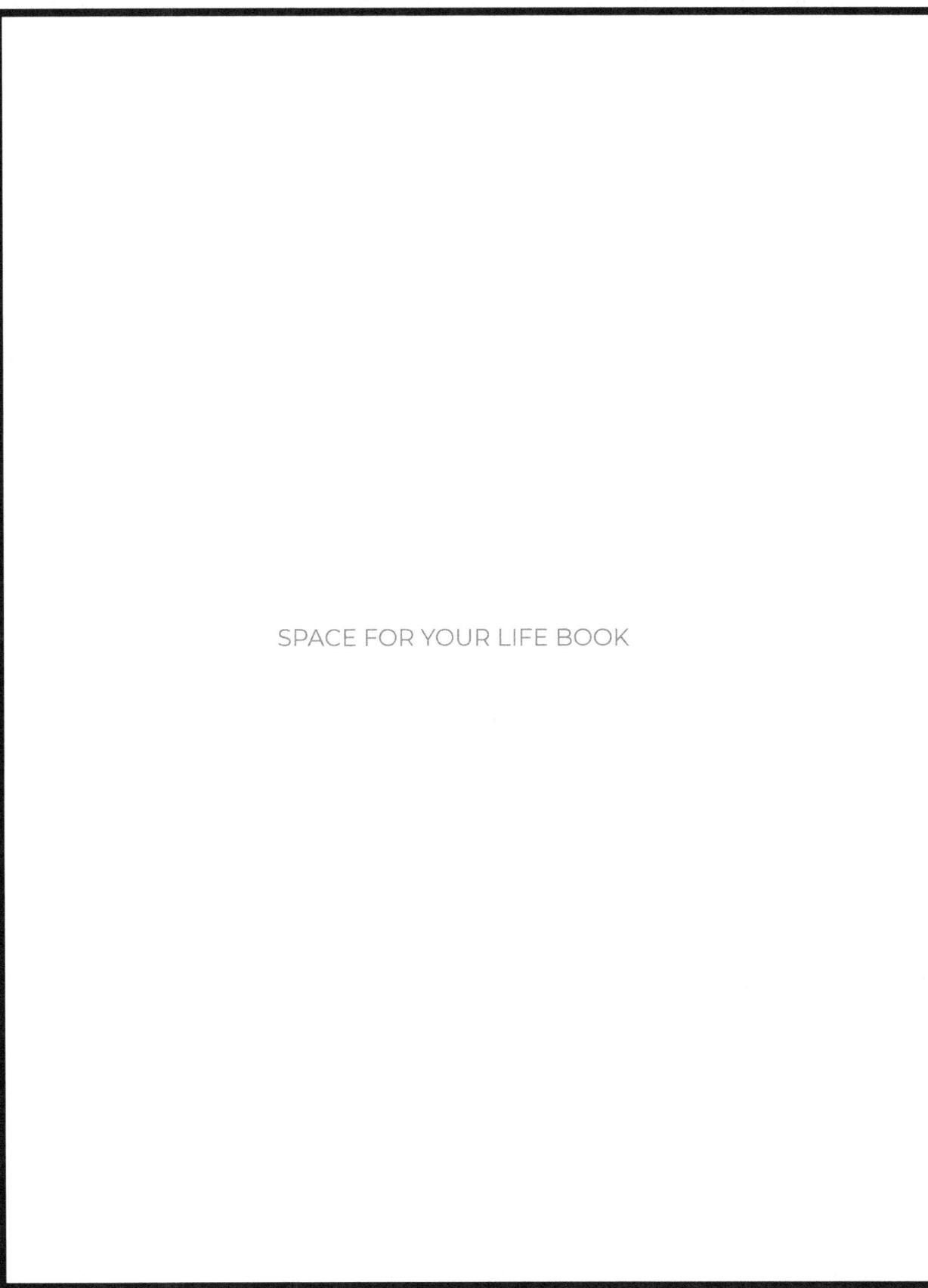

SPACE FOR YOUR LIFE BOOK

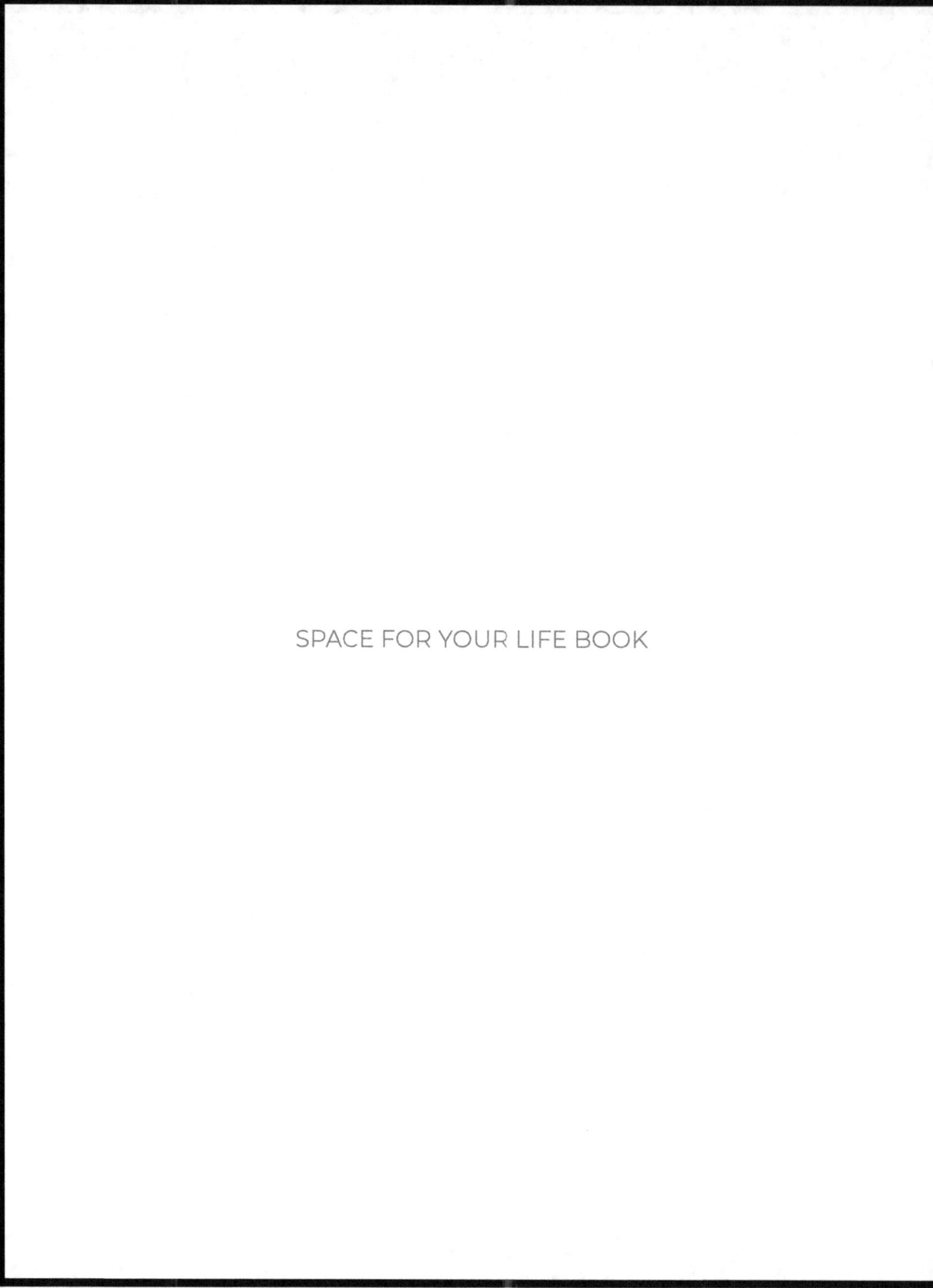

SPACE FOR YOUR LIFE BOOK

SPACE FOR YOUR LIFE BOOK

DID YOU KNOW. . . .

Tiffany Haddish *famous comedian and actor*
Simone Biles *Olympic & World Champion Gymnast*
Malcom X *powerful Civil Rights Leader*
Ice T *famous rapper*

ALL GREW UP IN FOSTER CARE?

They are proof that it <u>does not</u> matter where you start!
All your dreams are possible if you work hard and
BELIEVE in **YOURSELF.**

ANYTHING IS POSSIBLE
IF YOU
BELIEVE

Mark 9:23

For I know the plans I have for you, declares the Lord, plans for welfare and not for evil, to give you a future and a hope.

Jeremiah 29:11 (ESV)

CAN YOU **SEE** IT?

A vision board is a great way to keep track of the goals you want to accomplish! Think about your goals and dreams, then find pictures, statements, or words in a magazine or newspaper that represent each goal you have! Be as creative as you like and use the space below to create your vision board! If you want, you can make a large vision board using a posterboard and insert a picture of your board below.

And now, dear brothers and sisters, one final thing. Fix your thoughts on what is true, and honorable, and right, and pure, and lovely, and admirable. Think about things that are excellent and worthy of praise.

Philippians 4:8 (NLT)

POSITIVE SELF TALK

There is so much power in your words! When you are feeling down, it is easy to say negative things like, "I am not worth anything. I am a failure. I will never get this right." Challenge yourself to say positive things about yourself no matter how you feel. Write I AM statements that you will speak daily. A few are already listed just for you! Once you are done, write your statements on index cards and tape them to your mirror. Say them every morning as you prepare for your day!

I AM POWERFUL!
I AM SMART!
I AM ABLE TO DO SOME THINGS WELL!

PLAN SOME **FUN**

What activities do you enjoy? Use this calendar to schedule fun things you will do this month. You can even do one small fun thing everyday!

MONTH:			
SUNDAY	MONDAY	TUESDAY	WEDNESDAY

You don't have to have fun alone! Who would you like to join you for some fun this month?

THURSDAY	FRIDAY	SATURDAY

FUN! FUN! FUN!

10 RANDOM ACTS OF **KINDNESS**

Being kind to others helps us to feel better about ourselves. It makes God happy when His children stop and take a moment to show kindness to each other. Here are ten ways you can show kindness. Can you think of more? Find a way to be kind to someone everyday.

1. Give someone a compliment
2. Offer a hug
3. Smile at someone
4. Encourage a friend
5. Do a favor for someone
6. Give someone a gift
7. Open a door for someone
8. Bake cookies and share them
9. Give a thank you card
10. Call someone and tell them something nice

For God bought you with a high price. So you must honor God with your body.

1 Corinthians 6:20 (NLT)

EAT **HEALTHY**

Drinking water and healthy food like fruit and vegetables give us the energy we need to maintain positive self esteem. **What are some ways you can make sure you eat healthy everyday?**

Faith is taking the first step even when you don't see the whole staircase.

Dr. Martin Luther King Jr.

WORK IT OUT

Exercising builds our self-esteem. Being active at least 30 minutes a day makes us feel and look even better! **What are some of your favorite ways to be active?**

The more that you read, the more things you will know.
The more that you learn, the more places you'll go.

Dr. Seuss

READING IS FUN!

Reading a good book can help us learn new things and even use our imagination. **In the space below, write about a good book you've read! Be sure to include the title, author, and what you loved about it.**

DID YOU KNOW. . . .

When we laugh and smile, we instantly start to feel better. Smile and laugh a lot, it won't cost you anything. Here are a few other great benefits of laughing and smiling!

1. Smiling makes others around us want to smile.
2. Laughing relaxes you when you are overwhelmed.
3. Smiling lets others know that we are friendly.
4. Laughing helps our immune system fight off diseases and sickness.
5. Smiling makes you look successful.
6. Laughing is contagious! Once you start, no one can stop!
7. Smiling helps you think positive thoughts even on bad days.
8. Laughing removes pain and aches from our body.
9. Smiling helps us have better relationships with others.

SMILE

LAUGH

SHOW JOY

A cheerful heart is good medicine, but a broken spirit saps a person's strength.

Proverbs 17:22 (NLT)

SMILE FOR ME

What makes you smile? Can you think of a few silly jokes or a fun story? In the space below, **share a couple of things that put a smile on your face.**

Family and friends are hidden treasures, seek them and enjoy their riches.

Wanda Hope Carter

FAMILY & FRIENDS

It feels great to know that there are people who love and care for us! Spending time with our family and friends boosts our self-esteem and gives us the strength to meet our goals and chase our dreams. Insert pictures of you and your family and friends doing something fun below!

Give thanks to the Lord, for he is good! His faithful love endures forever.

Psalm 136:1 (NLT)

BE **THANKFUL**

We may not have everything we want, but we have a lot to be grateful for. When we take a moment to think about everything we are thankful for, we realize that life is not as bad as it may seem. Use the space below to write all the things you are grateful for!

Be free and express yourself. Do what comes naturally.

Cee Lo Green

EXPRESS YOURSELF

Writing is a great way to get our feelings out and express ourselves. There are so many things we can write! We can write a poem, a letter, or a short story about something we imagine. We can even write about our day. **In the space below, write something to express how you feel!**

Whatever is good and perfect is a gift coming down to us from God our Father, who created all the lights in the heavens.

James 1:17 (NLT)

YOU ARE **GIFTED**

You are great at alot of things! Take a moment and **write all of your strengths, talents, and gifts.** When you are done, give yourself a pat on the back for all the amazing things you can do!

A good teacher is like a candle – it consumes itself to light the way for others.

Mustafa Kemal Atatürk

A SPECIAL **TEACHER**

Teachers are unique people. They help us learn and grow. In the space below, **write about your favorite teacher!** You can even include a picture of that special teacher.

15 WAYS TO MANAGE NEGATIVE EMOTIONS

Everyone has emotions. We all experience happiness, sadness, joy, disappointment, and even anger. It's not bad to have emotions, and it is normal to experience negative emotions. We can not allow our emotions to make us do things we will regret later. Here are a few ways to manage negative emotions.

1. Punch a pillow
2. Take a shower
3. Go for a walk
4. Go to sleep
5. Listen to music
6. Talk to a friend or family member
7. Pray
8. Count to 10, 20 or 100
9. Scream
10. Journal
11. Take a jog
12. Walk away from the situation
13. Read
14. Cry
15. Take deep breaths

IT IS OKAY TO HAVE
EMOTIONS

BUT <u>DO NOT</u> LET YOUR EMOTIONS
HAVE YOU

Just try new things. Don't be afraid. Step out of your comfort zones and soar, all right?

Michelle Obama

TRY SOMETHING **NEW**

When we challenge ourselves to try something new, we gain confidence in ourselves. Have you ever wanted to try something new? What are somethings, places, or foods have you never experienced but always wanted to try?

You don't have enough faith," Jesus told them. "I tell you the truth, if you had faith even as small as a mustard seed, you could say to this mountain, 'Move from here to there,' and it would move. Nothing would be impossible."

Matthew 17:20 (NLT)

DO YOUR **CHORES**

Chores can be so boring. Who wants to spend all day cleaning, washing dishes, or organizing the closet? No one really, but here's the thing. When we take care of our chores, we learn how to be responsible. Also, it's a lot easier to have fun when everything is nice and neat! **What chores are you responsible for doing?**

Be kind to one another, tenderhearted, forgiving one another, as God in Christ forgave you.

Ephesians 4:32 (ESV)

CHOOSE TO **FORGIVE**

When we choose to forgive, we choose to no longer be angry with someone for doing something we didn't like. Forgiveness is hard, but it helps us feel better. Forgiving someone does not mean that they were not wrong for their actions. Forgiving means that you choose to no longer think about it, move on, and enjoy your life. Is there someone you need to forgive? Use the space below to write a letter to them. Tell them how you feel and let them know that you have chosen to forgive them. You don't have to share this letter with them if you don't want to. Forgiveness is a personal decision. If you are having a hard time forgiving, ask God to help you.

And I am sure of this, that he who began a good work in you will bring it to completion at the day of Jesus Christ.

Philippians 1:6 (ESV)

CERTIFICATION OF **COMPLETION**

This certifies that

_____

has completed The *I am a Masterpiece* **Workbook! Congratulations!**

Kimberly Purnell - Moody
_____   _____
Workbook Creator   date

ABOUT **THE AUTHOR**

Kimberly Moody is a former Child Welfare Social Worker, with over 20 years of Experience in Foster Care, Adoption and Post Adoption.

She is a graduate of East Carolina University and a member of **Alpha Kappa Alpha Sorority.**

She is the recipient of the 2000 Adoption Award from the State of North Carolina In appreciation for opening her heart to adoption and making a difference in the lives of children. She has been a presenter at various workshops including the North Carolina Division of Social Services Post Adoption Conference in 2007 and 2008. She has also partnered with Wendy's to host "Adoption Awareness Day" at local Wendy's Restaurants in Eastern North Carolina.

Kim currently lives in Winterville, NC with her husband and children. She is also A "MiMi." Both of her children were "handpicked" by God to join her family Through adoption!

FACEBOOK	Kimberly P. Moody
WEBSITE	www.kimberlypmoody.com
EMAIL	kimberlypurnellmoody@gmail.com

www.ingramcontent.com/pod-product-compliance
Lightning Source LLC
Chambersburg PA
CBHW081008120626
46546CB00010B/3065